MY HEART GOES
SWIMMING

my heart goes swimming

NEW ZEALAND LOVE POEMS

EDITED BY
JENNY BORNHOLDT
AND GREGORY
O'BRIEN

GODWIT

We're grateful to Roma Potiki, whose poem provided the title for this collection, and to Iain Sharp for allowing us to hijack his poem 'The enlistment' and use it as an envoi for this book. Thanks also to Marion McLeod, Bill Manhire, designer Sarah Maxey, and Jane Connor and Nicola Hill at Godwit.

Published by Godwit Publishing Ltd
15 Rawene Road, P.O. Box 34-683
Birkenhead, Auckland, New Zealand

First published 1996, reprinted 1996

ISBN 0 908877 81 1

Design and illustrations by Sarah Maxey
Typeset by Kate Greenaway
Printed by GP Print, Wellington

CONTENTS

ENVOI

If you know about clothing,
if you know about emptiness,
if you know clocks, drums, jigsaws,
if you know a secret,
if you know someone who knows,
even if you only
imagine that you know,
if you know you do not know,
if you do not know anything,
but will risk knowing me,
enter swiftly.
The archway never closes.
The century is ending.

INTRODUCTION

When trying to find love poems to read at a wedding in May 1994, we were struck by how hard it was to locate suitable New Zealand material — a problem accentuated by the absence of any compilation of recent indigenous love poetry.* The thought of putting together such a book crossed our minds a few weeks later when Vincent O'Sullivan asked Jenny for a copy of her unpublished 'Wedding Song' to read at a wedding.

Reading subsequently through New Zealand poetry, we were soon unearthing a wealth of love poems which we found accomplished, surprising and moving.

This selection is unashamedly a very personal one. Virtually all of the poems are celebratory — many could be read out at weddings and occasions. While some poems of loss and regret are included, we have avoided verse that embodied a cynical or disaffected view of love, as well as the kind of poetry — not infrequent up until the 1970s — that seemed intent on casting women as either Medusa figures or helpless beauties. A far larger, more inclusive anthology than this would be needed to contain the multitude of poems about frustrated / ruined / disastrous / cruel love.

Revelling in, and reflecting on, the possibilities of language as well as love, the poems vary from pensive to rapturous, from entertaining to plaintive, and from raucous

---

* Reading through James Bertram's 1977 anthology, *New Zealand Love Poems*, only made us more aware of the need for an up-to-date compilation, one which reflected the shifting social, political and personal mores of the last two decades.

9

to quiet. Some of them are written from an earthy perspective, while others — for instance Charles Brasch's 'Signals' and Eileen Duggan's 'The Tides run up the Wairau' — are imbued with notions of spiritual love. At times the tone can be gently ironic and subversive, as in Bill Manhire's 'My Sunshine', which the poet says is about 'a young man who — in the current jargon — has been constructed by the discourse of romantic love, and who finally runs out of words, even the comforting noises of popular song. . .'

We have arranged the book roughly according to the age we imagined the writer to be when they wrote each poem, although we've taken liberties here and there, shuffling some of the poems to get illuminating juxtapositions and make the book more readable, we hope, from beginning to end. Accordingly, the collection begins with poems about 'young love' — by writers as diverse as Paola Bilbrough (born 1971), Katherine Mansfield (born 1888) and a youthful Sam Hunt — then gradually the voices mature until, by the conclusion of the volume, the tone is predominantly melancholy and retrospective — a mood embodied in James K. Baxter's majestic 'He Waiata Mo Te Kare', which closes the collection.

We hope we have created a companionable book, one fitting to its subject — pleasing to both mind and ear, and capable of reaching the heart.

Jenny Bornholdt & Gregory O'Brien

WHEN SHE SPEAKS

Lovelier are her words
Than the exquisite notes
That speak the souls of flutes.
The songs of birds

At dusk, when the first-born star
Swims in the willow tree,
Are not more dear to me
Than her words are.

When she speaks, all sound begins
To tremble and melt
In music rarer than the lilt
Of violins.

Her voice is more delicate
Than the croon of wind in the coppice;
All the world's songs are poppies
Under her feet.

A. R. D. Fairburn

PAVILION

The house was in the mountains,
Perched on the moon's wrist.
We sung, we sang.
I have forgot it.

All day you drew ladies dancing on clouds,
One falling into the open mouth of a book.
It was in the mountains
And I prayed for the swan.
I forget it.

The red pavilion, the red pavilion.
A tree climbed back in its leaves.
Love, good morning,
Your body was all freckles.

Bill Manhire

SINGING FOR YOU NOW

I'd rambled on, uncertain of
My songs, vague memories of love,
   Sung them two years now,
When really knowing nothing more
Than empty bottles round the floor;
   Waking, doomed, at noon.

But then two months ago you came
Bringing me your childlike calm,
   Something wholly new —
To wake up with the first light breaking
Through your dark, lashed eyes; and making
   Love, not song, to you.

   And now I gather you
Dry firewood and flowers from the cliff,
And lastly this, this song plucked live
   From silence, love,

   Singing for you now.

Sam Hunt

VIGNETTE — SUMMER IN WINTER

Through the wild, Winter afternoon, Carlotta, at the piano, sang of Love.

Standing by the window, I watched her beautiful passionate profile. The walls were hung with daffodil silk. A faint golden light seemed to linger on her face. She wore a long black frock, and a hat with a drooping black feather. Her gloves, her great ermine coat, her silver purse were flung on the lounge beside her. The air was faintly scented with the perfume she loved that Winter — Peau d'Espagne.

There was a little fire of Juniper logs burning in the grate, the flames cast into the room strange, ghost-like shadows that leapt upon the curtains, upon the walls, that lurked behind the chairs and behind the lounge, that hid in the corners and seemed to point long shadow fingers at Carlotta.

She sang and sang, and the room seemed warm and full of sunshine and happy flowers. 'Come,' her voice cried to me, 'and we shall wander in a mystic garden filled with beautiful unexistent flowers. I alone possess the key. I alone can search out the secret paths. Lo there is a bower lit with the pale light of gardenia flowers . . . there are fountains filled with laughing water.'

I drew back the heavy curtain from the window. The rain was lashing against the glass. The house opposite appalled me — it was like the face of an old, old man drowned in tears. In the garden below rotting leaves were heaped upon the lawns and walks. The skeleton trees rattled together, and the wind had torn a rose bush from the ground. It sprawled across the path ugly and thorn-encrusted. Drearily, drearily fell the Winter rain upon the dead garden, upon the skeleton trees . . .

I turned from the window, and in the warm firelit room, with almost a note of defiance in her voice, Carlotta, at the piano, sang passionately of Love.

Katherine Mansfield

SALT

The woman with clocks and wrist watches on her stockings is sailing through a maze of islands. They are so close together and their edges so soft that the rudder of her boat slices pieces off in passing.

Every day she is gone he cleans a landscape of salt from her windows. Leaning against the refrigerator he is unsure about missing her. He eats a banana, enjoys watching his reflection in the flank of the kettle, the muscle working in his jaw. He would like to roll his body through each room like a carpet, richly patterned, resilient to the touch.

Outside he is the only one moving on an afternoon which has forgotten the time. He cleans the woman's windows, alternately rough then gentle. Swinging the water in great arcs, then dabbing the pane with a sponge, as if he were removing a moustache of milk from around a mouth.

Paola Bilbrough

INVENTING YOU

if I were to forget
the way I think of you
break you to bits
jumble you up
and sweep away all sign of you
and then if I were to start
all over again
and invent you
with nothing more to work on
than a notion
of your waiting to be discovered
I would not approach the problem
by trying to make you solid
giving you shape
attaching so many yards
of pretended skin
to so much meat and bone

the museums are full
of lively examples
of that kind of solution
but when the attendants
are not looking
my touch detects stone

instead
I would take silence

and begin with one sound
then another
to fill first the air
and the seas and the forests
then the towns
with your softness
if I were to forget
the way I think of you
and then invent you
all over again
I would assemble you
from sigh and laughter
from half-words and half-cries
from heartbeat
the click of bone

breathing in and breathing out
from all sound of true love
even the rub the skin makes
touching in sleep

Kevin Ireland

EARLY
MORNING
BUS

Lady
you & me
better
move
or we
may never
get
   to talk.
You might
lie
in the bay
cemetery
so
might I
under
the long grass
& still
more
than a stone's throw
   away.

Graham Lindsay

SONG OF CONSEQUENCES

You are in the house
   moving from room to room
      dropping articles of clothing

after you.
   I lift them and read
      the inner shapes of them,

your body's shapes,
   the sea and the mountain
      the running waves and the hard stones

the length of your arm
   the stretch of your leg,
      each room brings me closer

to the window
   where you sit naked
      halfturned to the inner light of the lamp

halfturned to the outer
   light of the pink sky, between both,
      a nakedness to lean into and touch

piece by piece
   putting all the pieces back
      in their places of belonging

here and here,
   simply, you turn and you smile
      at this, this touch of recognition.

Murray Edmond

SHIFT

Just home from work
in a rich hotel
where the windows don't open
she takes off her clothes
she leaves them where
they fall. The day is over

over & over & over
it explodes gently open.

Outside
the harbour
gleams. Foams like a
dream of apples. Like the windows

of a drowned hotel.

Bob Orr

AZTEC NOON

This I had thought forgotten
I recall now almost perfectly
In the gloom of winter:

Past a cloacal wall whose posters
Decayed like leonine faces,
I took you home up steps,

Strewn with crates and cabbage,
To a room which seemed a tank of light
At the very top of the world.

All summer was a gala Aztec noon
We walked in, hip to hip,
Through odour of the sea's green cistern.

Geoff Cochrane

AND MY HEART GOES SWIMMING

and my heart goes swimming

wet and lipid it hangs between waves of salt.
a warm heart in cold green waters
deep
to the bottom.

wave after wave washing the little skin
saline.

and my heart goes swimming

a fisherman scoops the sea,
finds a heart in his hand.

no cold fish warm red blood black hair
blonde.

a night of swimming,
open eyes laugh
see us
love
the man and my heart celebrate

and in the morning warm water from a tap.

but now the fisherman has fish to catch
see, he has a net, and sinkers.

back

to the sea
my heart goes swimming
wave after wave

no cold fish could swim like my heart goes swimming.

Roma Potiki

RANGITOTO/CANOE

In your room we are wrapped by the sound
of the sea,
by the redness your curtains make.
There is a green canoe on the lawn
which your father made out of demolition
timber the year he retired.
We make our love
and we ride it through the waters
of the room, hardly
needing to push it out but just
setting it out, watching it go as if
we ourselves were not in it
but two strangers putting out to sea
in each other's arms.
They would think they were lucky
or even blessed, not knowing all
the while that it was us. Not needing
to touch anything but the shore of a
known outline — your hip, my side,
where the ribs press out

the skin.
To be lost for an hour in a landscape
where many paths lead to different
coves, or as the case may be
a wide sweep of bay where clumps
of heedless lilies grow.

This I know for I have landed
on this outline, this hip of yours,
this arm, this knee — the small bend
where the green kidney ferns grow.

And none of it is more astounding
than the whole of you,
your heart, your penis — swimming
beneath your skin.
(The water) ah yes this morning
I can see through it,
see clear through to the bottom.

Virginia Were

THE TIDES RUN UP THE WAIRAU

The tides run up the Wairau
That fights against their flow.
My heart and it together
Are running salt and snow.

For though I cannot love you,
Yet, heavy, deep, and far,
Your tide of love comes swinging,
Too swift for me to bar.

Some thought of you must linger,
A salt of pain in me,
For oh what running river
Can stand against the sea?

Eileen Duggan

BON VOYAGE

to Meg

Crossing the straits is easy
As sleeping with you, my sweet:
The waves just keep slipping away
Like the bedclothes from our feet.

A salt moon leans to the mast,
White as your head on my arm —
I'm afraid of the lights on the sea,
I'm afraid of the calm.

A gull falls away in the dark,
Like your lost hand under a sheet
When hunger is deep as the ocean
And there's no advance or retreat.

Drowning is easy, my darling,
As when foundering lip to lip
Horizons topple and vanish
And into your breathing I slip.

Alistair Te Ariki Campbell

THE SOUNDS

Rain, a restful place: a plain
negotiation led to this, one small
lit room, in lieu of a camera, and the
drowned valleys, windless, listening
to the rain, on leaf, on water
in winter. Disentangled thus, we touch

as if deciphering a prophecy, we touch
as ocean, held by the land, made plain
a difficult map, whose cove-smooth water
uncoils with travel, surrounds a small
arrival, a larger departure. Listening
to the sounds as we pronounce them, the

waves, the bright particulars, we hear the
way we've been so far, we touch
speech, our bodies fearless listening
devices. And days unravel as on a plain
a road will travel straight with small
perceptible corrections. But water

under the hand of the wind, and water
in darkness: things we see and cannot tell, the
sounds are full of these too, as small
fish, late, in a bell of light, touch
the surface once and disappear. It's plain
each morning, talking and not listening

how plain things aren't, how whether we're listening
or not, the sounds go on around us, and water
will erase all previous arrangements. It's plain
how prophecies succumb before the
evidence, words in sand that crumble at a touch,
that need to be unwritten or forgotten, and small

reliable ambitions fashioned, parts for a small
cast — two, who move from stage to stage, listening
to the places where their different futures touch.
Rain-fast, a stream falls, to clear salt water
where just such a lean crew rows, the
dinghy iffing and butting, a plain

afternoon. The small boat drums the mingling water;
the rowers, listening, will remember the
sounds, when they touch, that these days made plain.

Andrew Johnston

THE LEGEND OF MARCELLO MASTROIANNI'S WIFE

All summer in the shallow sea
She lay on a lilo waiting
Dangling a hand, primed to embrace
And bless the demi-god.
She would cook from the freezer
Breasts of pasta, sauces like milk
Spoon-feed him, flirt
Mountainously and save herself.
In bed while she ministered
Territories of herself she spoke
Into the darkness the litany she'd learnt:
Whales, dolphins, the dove-like sea.

Elizabeth Smither

THE RING IS LOVELY

slender, dull silver
but I think it only
lovely when you hold it

Elizabeth Nannestad

CRIKEY

I can't think straight
my words spin off
in sugar & spice
god you're nice
I've got a running filmstrip
in my head of you
every time I close my eyes
I close my eyes quite often
I feel so good
I feel like a morning
a kiss on a ferris wheel
in the tunnel of love

I'm not quite sure what's happening
but your image is in me like a scent
all the roses in the garden are opening up at once
it's raining big round drops
of extraordinary sweetness
let me be serious
I'm in love with you
                    I think of
you at every
            turn   move
my hand
        your eyes   your
hand
    crikey

                do the washing
                                dream on the doorstep
clean all the windows at high speed
get lost
        stare into space
                                watch a

green caterpillar
spinning enough
amazingly fine
silk
to let itself down
smoothly
from the
very top
leaf
of the tree.

Cilla McQueen

RUTH

1

If I call you Ruth. She lay
at the big man's
feet & covered them.
Charity flowed from him
like good sense. He had cut
corn all day, dirt
filled his body's flaws, he
snored. I have not

so much as stepped
outside the front door.
The sound of wind in the cypress trees
is like you turning over.
If your breath
touched my face now I would
not call you Ruth. You
are not here. You are Ruth.
You looked back two or
three times trying
not to cry. This vacant image

is with me, the
knowledge of your absence,
a space you turn towards
doubtfully, having no choice.

The rest I
grope my hands through
like latticework, the negative

light in which my eyes
blaze, pearly cataracts.
There are things you
touched, they have gone.
My lips move upon a word, *Ruth.*
You are trees, a sound. You turn
to me with a sound
of wind stirring the cypress trees.
Your breath touches my face.

2

The blood rose out of me
for some who had not died
in makeshift ambulances along the
pitted Damascus road. I remembered

an evening in that white city
when my blood rose towards
you. Kites hung in the summer convections.
Your pale body on the white bed, long

scars across it, green jalousie shadows.
My life crowds up in me.

My thoughts tug like
kites above the dry upward currents.

3

Night wind in the dusty
cypress trees. No part of you
is whole to me, my blood rises for the wind
turning in my bed. Ideograms

of the blind, the violence of memory.
In the light cast upward
beyond your white body your tongue
is a dark fuse your eyes are
touched with red. You grip
me & tread my body drawing
blood. Each dove-twilight, each
morning they have brought up
mangonels against your tower-cote.
You turned sadly towards a
space, each morning
something more of you has gone.
It does not atrophy, I

cannot hold it, your image grows
into what surrounds me. *Ruth*
Ruth how long before
you cover me again,

simple & small as something done.
The red factor canary turns
out its wings, the cat goes daintily
across the garden, the
wind touches my face.

Ian Wedde

TURNING BROWN AND TORN IN TWO

You — a perfect reproduction
after a long day.
Smooth — folding through thin air
like a dart.

You lean against a wall
dropping leaves
or laughter — your eyes
lined with titles.

Is it not amazing
the way fingers filter down
— that tracing clipclip
of the runout groove.

It is barely an idea
how skin sails across the body
— a sheet of paper, warm
as a fresh photocopy.

James Brown

TRYST

Lie at twilight down amongst the grass.
Let the brown gorse stoop above you there.
Let the crushed fern tangle in your hair,
Close beside a road where few men pass.
Breathe the scent of little, earthly things.
Let the twilight touch you, breast and brow,
As a harper, leaping listful strings,
Tells the gleam of star-flowers withered now.
Drink the cup of silence deep for me,
Knowing that my spirit stands beside.
Let the purple dusk, the lover sea,
Beauty's passion, take you for a bride.
Yet, if one beloved should be near,
If his lips be tender on thy hair,
Take the hour, nor think my ghost must tread
Home on lonely ways with bended head.
For to-night, forgetting ancient bars,
I am master over wind and stars.
I can make the dying clover sweet —
Charm the stars like blossoms round your feet;
Lips that kindle into holy speech
Whisper but again the words I teach;
Arms that hold you give you but again
Shadow of our splendour and our pain.
Lie at twilight, where the grasses twine...
Life's long kiss against your eyes is mine.

Robin Hyde

AT LAST

Grey skies? No matter.
In the pet shop aviary
the small birds chatter.

The new butterflies
brush wings, mate on the lampshade.
The wind softly sighs.

A new moon will shine
with shy benevolence on
your body and mine.

Oh, my love, my love.
We form a single shadow.
We are hand in glove.

Iain Sharp

POEM

A puriri moth's wing
lies light in my hand —

my breath can lift it

light as this torn wing
we lie on love's breath.

Jan Kemp

LOVE POEM

There is no question
of choice, but it takes
a long time.

Love's vacancies, the eye
& cavity, track
back to embraces

where the spine bends
& quietens
like smoke in the earth.

Your tongue, touching on song,
darkens all songs. Your touch
is almost a signature.

Bill Manhire

The foreign city of two minds
is my home.   You and I had it pretty much
covered
        on foot on ferries on buses which made connections
eventually
            and while we waited and ate and swam away
went the fall in america   breathing
space for the future
                        delicate minutiae
of one mind made up
                    and coming true in the other.

Michele Leggott

But you
love I
knew by
heart

Wystan Curnow

MY LOVE LATE WALKING

My love late walking in the rain's white aisles
I break words for, though many tongues
Of night deride and the moon's boneyard smile

Cuts to the quick our newborn sprig of song.
See and believe, my love, the late yield
Of bright grain, the sparks of harvest wrung

From difficult joy. My heart is an open field.
There you may stray wide or stand at home
Nor dread the giant's bone and broken shield

Or any tendril locked on a thunder stone,
Nor fear, in the forked grain, my hawk who flies
Down to your feathered sleep alone

Striding blood coloured on a wind of sighs.
Let him at the heart of your true dream move,
My love, in the lairs of hope behind your eyes.

I sing, to the rain's harp, of light renewed,
The black tares broken, fresh the phoenix light
I lost among time's rags and burning tombs.

My love walks long in harvest aisles tonight.

James K. Baxter

GREEN

Dressed in green she came
  and like a tulip
leaned her head against the door
  and looked at me.
Her hand lay cool as a stone
    against her dress
    and her sandalled feet
showed white as a pair of doves
    on grass.
  She did not stir
but wanted me to speak to her.
    Her words
were lilies on a green stem
  the small wind shakes.

Alistair Te Ariki Campbell

ARIEL

Something that rises
beneath the curved
ribs, catching the
updraft of vision.
Unending kite
on the string
of love.

Bob Orr

THINE OWN HANDS HAVE FASHIONED

(poem for male and female voice)

O let the vain sun die
* with a peacock flourish*
so that I may rise from
* my labours and hasten*
to light up the dark tent
* that is . . . Delilah*

Beloved
            thine hands are distraught winds
            waking the dead cymbalic reeds
            at the edge of the lake.
            Hear ye the sullen moan of
            yielding trees
            the forlorn sighs of tormented hills
            the liquid gasp of molten valleys.

At your coming
            the surface of the moonless lake
            stiffens . . .

Beloved
            thine hands tongue an unalien speech
            with a maddening reticence:
            thine ostrich hands my lord
            are insultingly deaf to the pulsing
            clangour of the blood

and the urgent bell.
Rend them!
Destroy thy belltower of love.
Plunder thy storehouse of spices.

My lord
        thine hands drop with golden flowers
        from the lion's maw:
        thine hands contain the splendid fire
        of poised lances:
        they are exquisite pinnacles
        of light O lord . . .

Hear me
        I beseech thee
        when eagle screams fly up
        and a thousand gleaming spears
        impale the skies
        in the mounting savagery and
        the lull . . .

My lord my love
        . . . your hands are beautiful

Hone Tuwhare

THE KISS

There we were — two people
and a lot of scenery.

I don't know what business
you had to kiss me — now

everyone is interested:
the low boughs of pohutukawa

the shoulders of sand and the marram,
our radiant moon.

Don't stop now — think
how we'd disappoint them.

Elizabeth Nannestad

THE PROMISE
(Prothalamium)

A tall lass looking forward to
her wedding day,
         as dusk falls
cool, beneath the falls,
in Whangarei,
        dreams
yesterdays'
tomorrows stay
in falling trails. . . .

They turn all white
to chestnut, and all
streams turn to flow; and
she falls
     back from a
          past
        into
the futures we shall know
and smiles within
December dusk,
this evening's summer light:
and promises
late day forever,
now
against the night.

Alan Riach

WEDDING SONG

Now you are married
try to love the world
as much as you love
each other. Greet it as your husband,
wife. Love it with all your
might as you sleep
breathing against its back.

Love the world, when, late at night,
you come home to find snails
stuck to the side of the house
like decoration.

Love your neighbours.
The red berries on their trampoline
their green wheelbarrow.

Love the man walking on
water, the man up a
mast. Love the light moving
across the *Island Princess*.

Love your grandmother when she tells you
her hair is three-quarters 'cafe au lait'.

Try to love the world, even when you discover
there is no such thing as   *The Author*
any more.

Love the world, praise
god, even, when your aerobics instructor
is silent.

Try very hard to love
your mailman, even though he regularly
delivers you Benedicto Clemente's mail.

Love the weta you find on the path,
injured by alteration.

Love the tired men, the burnt
house, the handlebars of light
on the ceiling.

Love the man on the bus who says
it all amounts to a fishing rod
or a light bulb.

Love the world of the garden.
The keyhole of bright green grass
where the stubborn palm
used to be,
bees so drunk on ginger flowers
that they think the hose water
is rain   your hair tangled in
heartsease.   Love the way,
when you come inside,
insects find their way out
from the temporary rooms of
your clothes.

Jenny Bornholdt

from IN YOUR PRESENCE

(*a song cycle*)

In love, what do we love
But to give and to receive
That love by which we live.

You, loved and known and unknown,
Are the one and only one
World I am chosen to dwell in.

I turn in your day and your night
Pivoting on one thought,
What we are and are not,

That love as evergreen mover
Is our always and our never,
Creator, destroyer, preserver.

*

In the true-knot of your arms
Lock me from the world's alarms;
   To that narrow room
   All kingdoms come.

Waking, dreaming, we shall rove
The warm lands and seas of love,
   And fear no winter there
   Nor anguish on the air,

While feather winds wave us on
Through time coming and time gone,
  Present to us now
  In the sealing of a vow.

*

I rove, you stay,
Each constant in our own way,
Revolving in the erratic circles we must
Trace from dust to dust.

Faithful, faithless,
What do such counters mean to us who confess
That each draws for life-blood the whole
Breath of the other's soul.

Charles Brasch

WHEN IN STILL AIR

When in still air the planets shake
Like springs about to flow,
A wind from off Australia
Is gathering to blow.

When the grey-warbler sings close in
Upon the driest noon,
A cloud brewed from the Tasman
Will bring a rainy moon.

And I who have my signs of you
Am weatherwise in vain.
Oh you are gale and wet to me,
But come, my wind and rain.

Eileen Duggan

WEIGHING UP THE HEART

Always, there are our hearts
to consider.
They are most
precious to us.

*

The heart is a means
of description.
It will locate
the sentiment.
Speak up
small red thing.

*

The heart is
the deciding factor.
Wave your arms around
see the sky bloom.

*

The heart lives
as a steady witness
within the body.
We would hope
for a rigorous
sympathy
for the heart to
remember
the reliable place
in which it dwelled.

*

Always refer back
to the heart.
It is where
the world
began.

Jenny Bornholdt

MĀTAI RORE AU

(tribe unknown)

Mātai rore au ki te taumata,
Te ngākau whakapuke tonu.
Me aha iho ka mauru ai,
Whiuwhiu kei te muri, kei te tonga?

LOVE SONG

On the hill tops I visit the snares
And my heart keeps surging up.
Oh how can I quiet my heart,
That is tossed from north to south?

(translated by Margaret Orbell)

from UTA

(free translations from Japanese classical collections)

We two
found it so hard
the Autumn mountain —
how will you
cross it alone?

*

Great ships
riding at anchor
are rocked
as I by my love
for this man-child.

*

Beautiful
he seems to me
like the swift river
dammed
and breaking through.

*

People
in this towered city
abound.
My heart
has only one inhabitant.

*

My lover
is thinly clad.
Wind of Sao
hold your breath
till he's home.

*

Meetings in dreams
are sad.
I wake
reach out
and touch nothing.

*

My little cloud
thunder-shot
with lightning —
seeing you, I'm afraid.
Seeing you go, I'm sad.

*

My hair this morning
I won't comb.
The hand
of my beautiful lord
has been its pillow.

*

Dim
the russet shore
in morning mist
among islands
where my thoughts pursue your skiff.

*

On this route
to nowhere
may the frontier guards
every night
sleep sound.

*

First light
flickers
in the east
and we fumble
to dress each other.

C. K. Stead

SEVEN WISHES

A straight account is difficult
so let me define seven wishes:

that you should fit inside me neat as the stuffing in an
    olive
that you should stand inside the safe circle of my eye
that you should sing, clear, on the high rock of my
    skull
that you should swing wide on the rope of my hair
that you should cross rivers of blood, mountains of
    bone
that I should touch your skin through the hole in your
    tee shirt
that we should exchange ordinary tales.

Fiona Farrell

LOVE BY CANDLELIGHT

Lift up your brown arms
    And let fall your heavy hair.
Here no one may enter
None climb the stair.

Bend down your ripe mouth.
    Love's fire-bright silence, this
Half-painful, shadow haunted
So-much-longed-for kiss.

Open your green eyes.
    Pin-points of candleshine
In caverns of coolness gleam
Here, close to mine.

Rest your dear head night-long
    In its accustomed place.
I seek no other heav'n
Beyond your mortal face.

Mary Stanley

NOT MADE WITH HANDS

Find me the rose that will not die,
The tree no axe can fell,
The spring no Summer's drought shall dry,
And this last miracle:
Show me the wood, the timeless wood
Where tall and steadfast stands
(The lightnings quenched, the storms withstood)
A house not made with hands.

Here is your rose that will not die,
Your tree no axe can fell,
The spring no Summer's drought shall dry,
And here your miracle:
Behold the wood, the timeless wood,
And see how, steadfast, stands
(All lightnings quenched, all storms withstood)
Love's house, not made with hands.

Ruth Gilbert

BIG HOUSES

I will put you in a big house
on a great estate
at the fresh end of summer

I will put you in a blue
dress, I will trick
you out in dazzling colour.

How else can I make you stay?
And you are always disappearing
anyway.   So:

I will put you on a red horse
with a white blaze
with a heart like a haybarn

pacing down the stopbank in a
downpour of cotton seed, scarlet
geranium / purple iceplant

all this glamorous
scenery riding up to meet you.
While you in the same breath ride

free of it. That is, you
have other ideas: you are always
somewhere else, being you.

John Newton

EVEN IN THE DARK

As a room you know,
And even at midnight
Walk through effortlessly,
By sense, not sight
Passing unscathed between
Table and chair
Avoiding the low foot-stool,
Faultlessly aware
Of ledge and bowl
Of flower and crystal vase;
Moving unerringly
Without fear or pause
To the desk with its open book,
Paper-knife, and book-mark:
As this room I would have you know me,
Even in the dark.

Ruth Gilbert

OUR LOVE WAS A GRIM CITADEL

Our love was a grim citadel:
    no tawdry plaything for the minute
    of strong dark stone we built it well
    and based in the ever-living granite:

The urgent columns of the years
    press on, like tall rain up the valley:
    and Chaos bids ten thousand spears
    run to erase our straw-built folly.

R. A. K. Mason

LOVE POEM

A woman comes into a room where a vase stands on a
    table.
The table is close against a wall, beside an open window,
so the vase might seem outside the window
against the trees, above a stretch of lawn,
for the merest second for the woman entering.
She walks to the vase to touch it, turns it a little,
rests her curved fingers on its curved rim,
inattentive to what she holds, to the fact of her hands,
although the vase is foreign and perfect,
                her hands what she is proud of.
She walks from the room, leaves table as table, window
as pure window — the world as it is.
Yet the lawn outside has altered, and the line of trees,
and the shadow of the line of trees on the shaven pallor
    of the lawn.
Although nothing has moved, all altered.
At every window, fictions.
                Love at each door.

Vincent O'Sullivan

THE CAVE

From the cliff-top it appeared a place of defeat,
the nest of an extinct bird, or the hole where the sea
    hoards its bones,
a pocket of night in the sun-faced rock,
sole emblem of mystery and death in that enormous
noon.

We climbed down, and crossed over the sand,
and there were islands floating in the wind-whipped
    blue,
and clouds and islands trembling in your eyes,
and every footstep and every glance
was a fatality felt and unspoken, our way
rigid and glorious as the sun's path,
unbroken as the genealogy of man.

And when we had passed beyond
into the secret place and were clasped
by the titanic shadows of the earth,
all was transfigured, all was redeemed,
so that we escaped from the days
that had hunted us like wolves, and from ourselves,
in the brief eternity of the flesh.

There should be the shapes of leaves and flowers
printed on the rock, and a blackening of the walls
from the flame on your mouth,
to be found by the lovers straying
from the picnic two worlds hence, to be found and
    known,
because the form of the dream is always the same,
and whatever dies or changes this will persist and
    recur,
will compel the means and the end, find
    consummation,
whether it be
silent in swansdown and darkness, or in grass
    moonshadow-mottled,
or in a murmuring cave of the sea.

We left, and returned to our lives:

the act entombed, its essence caught
for ever in the wind, and in the noise of waves,
for ever mixed
with lovers' breaths who by salt-water coasts
in the sea's beauty dwell.

A. R. D. Fairburn

THE GRIN

When I see a girl
quite absurdly happy
I think of you
coming to meet me.
Only those truly in love
smile that strange smile.
As a gannet,
wings fanned in the wind,
brakes on a nested rock
joyfully open-billed,
so I home in
to you with this wild grin.

Keith Sinclair

from THE GREEK ANTHOLOGY

That evening when we said goodnight
Moiris kissed me.
Did it really happen or
did I dream it?
I know the hour was seven.
I'm sure about everything else too —
what he said, our mirth.
But about the kiss
I'm really in the dark.
Because, if it truly did happen,
how is it after being in heaven
I'm wasting my time here on earth.

adapted by Ross Fraser

PER DIEM ET PER NOCTEM

Birds in their oratory of leaves
clamour at morning over my love.
All waters praise him, the sea harbours
from harm, all islands are his neighbour
and rain at daybreak feathers his peace
softer than pillows or my kiss.

O may his lucky hand at noon
pluck down the sun, all day his keen
eye be darkened by no cloud.
Sky-walker, the lonely hawk, applaud
his purpose, the equipoise among
cliff and rock, his difficult song.

O never may night confound or send
him lost into that hinterland
far from my coasts. Where is your moon,
Endymion, trimming her thin
flame to light my love? The world
lifts its shoulder to shelter him curled
in the lap of sleep. By falling star
I wish all his tomorrows fair.

Mary Stanley

from THE POEM THEN, FOR LOVE

And just now

The way light swarms over
your shoulders.
The day is remarkable that lifts
the town to walk on stilts.
The sun wheels down,
windows shine.

In the crowns of flowers
small fires leap; seeds spill
in the bright air.
Like planets spinning
into sight, passatempo our bodies
turn the hours.

For love your hair sings,
and earth's curve.
For love I pour light
into your body like this —
oh, there is music to be heard,
and just now.

Michael Harlow

A PROPOSITION

You have altered the contours of my dreams
All landscapes are peopled by you
All songs sing only of you.

But when all has been said and done
What then, my dear, what then?
Will our different winters
Thaw to the same spring,
Or will another ice-age grip
And hold us, separate, till the end?

The master plan is never ours
Nor the last word. This is all
We'll ever know or need to know.
Let us love each other now
As best we can. I fear
We may not have very long.

J. C. Sturm

from WATER, WOMEN AND BIRDS
GATHER

We'll be two still birds.
Silent.   Waiting.

An insect or a song?
Questions have no answers

until they are answered.
They make no sense

in a vague tilting emptiness.
Fill my voice with your voice!

We'll take the dregs of this day,
eat its creatures and sweeten it.

Your hand lies on my knee
as I write this love poem.

I forget you are there
and go — bereft — to the sea.

Thank heaven there's a kite
— exuberant — in the grey sky.

Look, you say later, in the garden,
take this violet. It has a slight,

unforgettable scent. Take it
in recollection of me.

Stay in the physical world you say.
Take your boots and socks off.

Be with me on the edge
of this body of water

and feel it come up
line after line.

Link arms with me in the sandhills.
Think only about the love

we are going to make
and how we are going to make it.

You'll be the windchime.
I'm the off-sea breeze.

Dinah Hawken

LIKE LAMPLIGHT

One day when you are beside me
invite me to speak
of the secrets I never knew
I wanted to tell you, of the warmth
I never knew I owned
until you released it
by moving close as lamplight seems
to glass. Ask me

why I came to you
with the reverence of one
who sees a flower bloom
where none has bloomed before.
By saying what is
I will have said what was.

Sometimes when you are content
ask me what it is
that moves me to want to hold you so,
so often, and laugh when I tell
you the same old
indestructible thing.

One day when you are
where you need no invitation to be
I will tell you
how you flower
like lamplight in me.

Brian Turner

SEE WHAT A LITTLE MOONLIGHT CAN DO TO YOU?

The moon is a gondola.
It has stopped rocking.
Yes. It's stopped now.

And to this high plateau
its stunning influence
on surge and loll of tides
within us should

somehow not go
unremarked
for want of breath
or oxygen.

And if I
to that magic micro-second
instant
involuntary arms reach out
to touch   detain

then surely
it is because you
are so good:
so very good to me.

Hone Tuwhare

MY SUNSHINE

He sings you are my sunshine
and the skies are grey, she tries
to make him happy, things
just turn out that way.

She'll never know
how much he loves her
and yet he loves her so much
he might lay down his old guitar
and walk her home, musician
singing with the voice alone.

Oh love is sweet and love is all, it's
evening and the purple shadows fall
about the baby and the toddler
on the bed. It's true he loves her
but he should have told her,
he should have, should have said.

Foolish evening, boy with a foolish head.
He sighs like a flower above his instrument
and his sticky fingers stick. He fumbles
a simple chord progression,
then stares at the neck.
He never seems to learn his lesson.

Here comes the rain. Oh if she were only
sweet sixteen and running from the room again,
and if he were a blackbird
he would whistle and sing
and he'd something
something something something.

Bill Manhire

BRIGHTNESS

I am bright with the wonder of you
And the faint perfume of your hair

I am bright with the wonder of you
You being far away or near

I am bright with the wonder of you
Warmed by your eyes' blue fire

I am bright with the wonder of you
And your mind's open store

I am bright with the wonder of you
Despite the dark waiting I endure

I am bright with the wonder of you.

Denis Glover

PARADOX

You so tender are so

rough, so coarse are so
delicate: if it were not so

you would not fit me.

Judith Lonie

from THE PHOTOGRAPH

. . . I'm
holding the round
magnifying
glass
on the park
the blurred image
steps into
detail.

the concert is over
the fanning wind
has emptied the
park.
they have taken
their time
over lunch,
reclining
a narrow river
of space
between them.
he has never taken
his eyes
off her face.
now the wine glasses
are back in the little
picnic hamper
the empty shoes

at angles
beside them (as in
the holy places)
while they settle
more comfortably
onto the plaid.
as she lies she
knots her hands
round his neck &
regards him.
he has never taken
his eyes
from her face.

Joanna Margaret Paul

THE HISTORY OF COCA-COLA

Hinting at something greater than itself
like a baby with a Winston Churchill
face you have one foot on earth
and another in heaven holding
the Jane Russell shaped bottle.

Even if the film's gauzy with age
and those fiery tracers are playing
for keeps arcing over the water
between good and evil you know
it made men out of those

leathernecks crossing the Rhine.
Now beyond the last billboard
between the sheets you want to know
what it is you're drinking —
you whisper your life in my ear

yes I remember our first date
yes I remember the first time
you took me in and now —
your smile like the light
from an open fridge.

Hugh Lauder

BEAUTIFUL GOLDEN GIRL
OF THE SIXTIES

Beautiful
golden girl of the Sixties
I remember your mouth
under the Pacific stars

I remember your delicate pale breast
in some dark old car backseat
the salt beachparty flavour of you in sandy tussock

I remember you stumble-drunk in an alley
& made clumsy by desire
in your very best dress

& the sound of summer after-work traffic on the hill
where you shared my narrow bed
when the night-scented datura lilies
began to breathe into the room
your thighs pale as lilies
their evening nectar

& how could you forget when
we managed it in the toilet
of the old clang-bang all-night Limited from Wellington
to Auckland, must've been dead of night
near frosty Taumaranui

oh ho beautiful golden girl of the Sixties

or the time at dawn in a narrow bunk
on the all-night ferryboat from Christchurch
to Wellington, & the tealady
never spilt a drop

Once on the top platform
of a slide in the children's playground
at birdsong dusk in Coromandel
in summer & someone nearby yelled out
'There's a time & place for everything!'
— quite right! And

I remember the elevator
of the hotel St George in Beirut
both of us crazy from separation at gunpoint
& that night parked in fresh pinegroves
above the city, a patrol with torches & machineguns
& us stark naked & covered with blood
from your nose that I'd knocked in fright
& I couldn't find my glasses

obvious we weren't spies
we were just investigating each other

hey beautiful golden girl of the Sixties

something we did also in hotpools & in cool rivers
& in baths & in showers & in the sea

in grass (often)
up in a tree (pohutukawa)
in sand

on floors, carpets, chairs, tables
in kitchens, dining rooms, living-rooms, lounges,
bathrooms
and in very many bedrooms

filled with woodsmoke & mosquitoes & the sound
of the sea or the sound
of city traffic or of wind, or opening wide windows
to the stars, the clouds

and in tents & combies &
hotel & motel rooms & in cheap spermy motorcamps
with the smells of last summer's crayfish dinner
round the cookhouse, piddle under the pines

oh oh beautiful golden girl of the Sixties

poor blanket student cot, green nikau palm arbour
car backseat, cool heaven of wide whitesheeted bed
Sri-Lankan resthouse, sexy Swiss featherbed
Tunisian bandit pinewood, dim cheap Damascus hotel
sad dark South London, sodden sheets in Denpasar
Otago winter quilts

maybe mostly the wide cool beds
where we lay heads together
talking when it was quiet

straight, drunk, stoned, stopped, speeding, tripped
sad, happy, tired, daytime, night, morning, hot, cold
fucking & tasting, your huge flavours & groan
our hands & mouths, your bubble saliva, my come
weary & gay, your smell, the bitter fuck of rage
in silence, with laughter, to music, meanwhile-conversation
'that was great' — 'that was terrible' — 'again' — 'later' —
your tongue, your eyes, your frightening tears
your giggle, your toughness, your smile
your shudder, your sardonic forbearing, your sudden sweat
your stoopid, your brave terror, your

your body where I dip my chipped cup
like a despairing pilgrim

ah 'my' beautiful golden girl of the Sixties

mother of my sons, your tired
lovely body where I bring my terminal need
where I stoop with cracked shaking lips

beatup puppydog cock, sad smile
& pounding heart, saying Show me again
this everyday miracle
how you bring forth such floods of seed from a fool

Ian Wedde

leap

(for Sue)

yes, let's

leap

into a

leaf

heap

Wystan Curnow

TWO OF US

    We total 2   That's quite okay
for such a ha ha day
walking down the Parade
to the floodgates
opened by a southerly   We skylark
The Inundation we proclaim
as it slams the Siren Rocks
High on a roof-top
Signor Tony de Gregorio is painting a house
'Hi Tony...
come down to the park'
    We leap the low ha-ha
A door falls from a tree
almost *taking the head off*
the local weirdo   We call
that an intervention
It takes all kinds in this weather
The wind eats me
standing up in my dimension
Do you remember the birds
in that marketplace?   Together
we purchased the incredible cloth
    I saw how you dressed this morning
Like a Highness of the Nile
before her specula   The hallucination
of a moth   *Ay!* from forth this ha ha day
the ministers decree

that copper coinage is illegal
Who would be the 1?
The surly sea repairs the way
we see   Tony paints *all*
the houses white   It's quite
a sight, o you say
and so are you   For coming out
    I thank you on such a ha ha day

Alan Brunton

ABOUT OURSELVES

In our separate lives
We unite
Not merely at meal-times
Or in bed in the illumined night.

Love lives on love and thrives
As it must indeed
On difference. Indifference
Is the prerogative of the dead.

Let's look to the now, looking
Trustingly ahead.
For we are two, yet one,
The moon being complementary
To the sun.

Which precedence has moon, has sun?
The heavens mystery
Is not for mortal woman or for man.

We only know what we have always
    known,
That without love we live alone.

Denis Glover

WIFE TO HUSBAND

From anger into the pit of sleep
You go with a sudden skid. On me
Stillness falls gradually, a soft
Snowfall, a light cover to keep
Numb for a time the twitching nerves.

Your head on the pillow is turned away;
My face is hidden. But under snow
Shoots uncurl, the green thread curves
Instinctively upwards. Do not doubt
That sense of purpose in mindless flesh:
Between our bodies a warmth grows;
Under the blankets hands move out,
Your back touches my breast, our thighs
Turn to find their accustomed place.

Your mouth is moving over my face:
Do we dare, now, to open our eyes?

Fleur Adcock

AFTER LOVING

While we lie hidden in ourselves
a moment longer, two colours
light up a world within.
At first, Chinese red
because we are happy,
and then emerald,
the god-green of peace
that follows when you follow me
while my hands
wing their separate flights
along your gullies.

Meg Campbell

EARTHQUAKE WEATHER

For three days now, the air
has been quiet and still.
Yesterday, a vase walked across
the mantelpiece. A friend and I
have traced the fault line
along a map. It is very close.
There is neither sun, nor yet rain,
and the wind has departed too.
The crickets have stopped singing
and the children's quarrels grown bitter.
We wait, sealed in this
grey vacuum.

And when we went to bed
last night, the moon slanted
between the curtains (yes,
we still have a moon),
catching your white smile
in a dazzling glitter. We
who have known rage and lust,
regrets and promises, have come
to understand love. I was afraid
you were about to devour me.
I wish this weather
would break soon.

Fiona Kidman

A LATE HONEYMOON

We are wearing exactly the clothes
for such summer expeditions —
practical, worn to dullness, confining:
the hats against the sun, the laced boots for walking,
our broadcloth statements about Nature.

Stranding here, a little separate
the rough ground of rocks and bushes between
we see the sea's blueness framed
by two grotesque pinnacles,
chalk at this distance glinting like ice

but ready to crumble obediently
under the master touch of winter rains.
Returning, we shall draw closer
on the downward path to the hotel
where white curtains billow by an open window.

We do not speak at all
feeling no need for conversation:
the afternoon holds us in its golden arms.
Tonight I shall write in my diary:
'Walked to clifftop with H. Fine view of sea.'

Such fantastic shapes the rain carves!
But you can't beat the sea for simplicity
and the statements of flat calm.
Look: far out, a breeze has caught two tiny sails
and draws them steadily to the white horizon.

Iain Lonie

THE MOUNTAIN

Oh love let us learn our love
now there is no more laughing in it —
let us remember the mountain
when we woke to the frost
and ran with our clothes to the kitchen,
airless and smelling of coal dust,
and dressed quickly in front of
the banked-up stove
glancing out at the glacier
gleaming on Girdlestone's shoulder . . .
and at night, how we stood
on the tiny porch together
and shook in the mazarine dark
and gasped and went in
shutting the door on the cold
and the mountain's terrible closeness.

Lauris Edmond

SIGNALS

No two bodies taste alike or smell alike.
Your cat will tell you so sooner than I can,
But not more certainly.

You are not what you were before we knew each other;
I cannot explain the difference, but
All my antennae report it.

Nor can I put my finger on the difference in myself
Now we have learned to answer signals
We did not receive once.

Your skin tastes and smells of tropics where I walked
Barefoot, nostrils wide and fingers
Winged over waves,

Where shadows drew me in through their like leafiness
That is yours now, leafy, woodier to taste
And salt with the salt we share insatiably,

Yours, mine, still distinguishable though mingled
As limbs are, as breathing is,
As tongues that taste each other.

Charles Brasch

SHE WAS MY LOVE WHO COULD DELIVER

She was my love who could deliver
From paws of pain and melancholy,
And light the lamps that burn forever,
And cleanse a page of screeds of folly,
And with a motion of her hand
Could heap a harvest on my land.

And she could melt an iron mood,
And lashing chords with love were softer,
And she could bring my course to good,
Could renovate with raining laughter,
And eye and heart her beauty brace
When death approached with peering face.

Against a secret shaft of malice
Piercing my solitary isle
She would defend with flying solace,
And visitations of her smile,
And from the spirit's blank occasions,
And from the craft of days and seasons
She was my love who could deliver.

J. R. Hervey

SEVEN MYSTERIES

Now write down
the seven mysteries:
why you so young and beautiful should die;
why consciousness prevents
escape into the chestnut branches where
foliage goes soft
with God's vermilion;
why what is said is seldom what was meant;
why men and women work, come home,
cook meals, argue and renew
their vows of silence or revenge;
why we were different;
why there are seven of everything;
why I go on
broken-winded like that horse we saw
on the ridge above Waipatiki
by a bent tree
watching the waves roll in.

Michael Jackson

THE GOLDEN FLOWER

Flower of gold, receive my love.
Hold it. Glow for me.
Take on a richer deeper hue.
Show me the depth of my love
For your beauty.
Golden flower,
Love has made you.
Become for me
So deep
So wonderful a flower
That I shall
Love you for your beauty alone.
You are not mine.
I only made you, golden flower.
Flower, free to love all,
Glow golden, more gold.
Become, flower of love,
The perfect flower.

Helen Shaw

HE WAIATA MO TE KARE

1

Up here at the wharepuni
That star at the kitchen window
Mentions your name to me.

Clear and bright like running water
It glitters above the rim of the range,
You in Wellington,
I at Jerusalem,

Woman, it is my wish
Our bodies should be buried in the same grave.

2

To others my love is a plaited kono
Full or empty,
With chunks of riwai,
Meat that stuck to the stones.

To you my love is a pendant
Of inanga greenstone,
Too hard to bite,
Cut from a boulder underground.

You can put it in a box
Or wear it over your heart.

One day it will grow warm,
One day it will tremble like a bed of rushes
And say to you with a man's tongue,
'Taku ngakau ki a koe!'

3

I have seen at evening
Two ducks fly down
To a pond together.

The whirring of their wings
Reminded me of you.

4

At the end of our lives
Te Atua will take pity
On the two whom he divided.
To the tribe he will give
Much talking, te pia and a loaded hangi.

To you and me he will give
A whare by the seashore
Where you can look for crabs and kina
And I can watch the waves
And from time to time see your face
With no sadness,
Te Kare o Nga Wai.

5

No rafter paintings,
No grass-stalk panels,
No Maori mass,

Christ and his Mother
Are lively Italians
leaning forward to bless,

No taniko band on her head,
No feather cloak on his shoulder,

No stairway to heaven,
No tears of the albatross.

Here at Jerusalem
After ninety years
Of bungled opportunities,
I prefer not to invite you
Into the pakeha church.

6

Waves wash on the beaches.
They leave a mark for only a minute.
Each grey hair in my beard
Is there because of a sin,

The mirror shows me
An old tuatara,
He porangi, he tutua,
Standing in his dusty coat.

I do not think you wanted
Some other man.

I have walked barefoot from the tail of the fish to the nose
To say these words.

7

Hilltop behind hilltop,
A mile of green pungas
In the grey afternoon
Bow their heads to the slanting spears of rain.

In the middle room of the wharepuni
Kat is playing the guitar, —
'Let it be! Let it be!'

Don brings home a goat draped round his shoulders.
Tonight we'll eat roasted liver.

One day, it is possible,
Hoani and Hilary might join me here,
Tired of the merry-go-round.

E hine, the door is open,
There's a space beside me.

8

Those we knew when we were young,
None of them have stayed together,
All their marriages battered down like trees
By the winds of a terrible century.

I was a gloomy drunk.
You were a troubled woman.
Nobody would have given tuppence for our chances,
Yet our love did not turn to hate.

If you could fly this way, my bird,
One day before we both die,
I think you might find a branch to rest on.

I chose to live in a different way.

Today I cut the grass from the paths
With a new sickle,
Working till my hands were blistered.

I never wanted another wife.

9

Now I see you conquer age
As the prow of a canoe beats down
The plumes of Tangaroa.

You, straight-backed, a girl,
Your dark hair on your shoulders,
Lifting up our grandchild,

How you put them to shame,
All the flouncing girls!

Your face wears the marks of age
As a warrior his moko,
Double the beauty,
A soul like the great albatross

Who only nests in mid ocean
Under the eye of Te Ra.

You have broken the back of age.
I tremble to see it.

10

Taraiwa has sent us up a parcel of smoked eels
With skins like fine leather.
We steam them in the colander.
He tells us the heads are not for eating,

So I cut off two heads
And throw them out to Archibald,
The old tomcat. He growls as he eats
Simply because he's timid.

Earlier today I cut thistles
Under the trees in the graveyard,
And washed my hands afterwards,
Sprinkling the sickle with water.

That's the life I lead,
Simple as a stone,
And all that makes it less than good, Te Kare,
Is that you are not beside me.

James K. Baxter

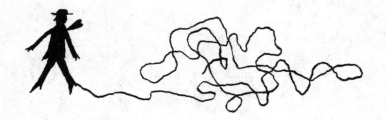

ACKNOWLEDGEMENTS

Godwit Publishing, Jenny Bornholdt and Gregory O'Brien gratefully acknowledge the following authors, publishers and literary agents for permission to include poems in this collection: Fleur Adcock and Oxford University Press for 'Wife to Husband'; the estate of James K. Baxter and Oxford University Press for 'My Love Late Walking' and 'He Waiata mo Te Kare'; Paola Bilbrough for 'Salt'; Jenny Bornholdt and Victoria University Press for 'Wedding Poem' and 'Weighing up the Heart'; the estate of Charles Brasch and Oxford University Press for extract from 'In Your Presence' and 'Signals'; James Brown and Victoria University Press for 'Turning Brown and Torn in Two'; Alan Brunton for 'Two of Us'; Alistair Te Ariki Campbell for 'Green' and 'Bon Voyage'; Meg Campbell for 'After Loving'; Geoff Cochrane and Victoria University Press for 'Aztec Noon'; Wystan Curnow for 'leap' and [but you love]; estate of Eileen Duggan for 'The Tides Run up the Wairau' and 'When in Still Air'; Lauris Edmond and Bridget Williams Books for 'The Mountain'; Murray Edmond for 'Song of Consequences'; the estate of A. R. D. Fairburn and Richards Literary Agency for 'When She Speaks' and 'The Cave'; Fiona Farrell and Auckland University Press for 'Seven Wishes'; Ross Fraser for extract from 'The Greek Anthology — an adaptation'; Ruth Gilbert for 'Not Made with Hands' and 'Even in the Dark'; the estate of Denis Glover and Richards Literary Agency for

'Brightness' and 'About Ourselves'; Michael Harlow and Auckland University Press for 'And just now'; Dinah Hawken for extracts from 'Water, Women and Birds Gather'; the estate of J. R. Hervey for 'She was my love who could deliver'; Sam Hunt for 'Singing for you now'; Kevin Ireland for 'Inventing You'; Michael Jackson and McIndoe Publishers for 'Seven Mysteries'; Andrew Johnston for 'The Sounds'; Jan Kemp for 'Poem'; Fiona Kidman and Random House for 'Earthquake Weather'; Hugh Lauder and Caxton Press for 'The History of Coca Cola'; Michele Leggott for [the foreign city of two minds]; Graham Lindsay for 'Early Morning Bus'; the estate of Iain Lonie and Victoria University Press for 'A Late Honeymoon'; the estate of Judith Lonie for 'Paradox'; Bill Manhire for 'Pavilion' and 'Love poem'; Bill Manhire and Victoria University Press for 'My Sunshine'; the estate of R. A. K. Mason and Richards Literary Agency for 'Our Love was a Grim Citadel'; Cilla McQueen and McIndoe Publishers for 'Crikey'; Elizabeth Nannestad and Auckland University Press for 'The ring is lovely'; Elizabeth Nannestad for 'The Kiss'; John Newton for 'Big Houses'; Vincent O'Sullivan and Oxford University Press for 'Love Poem'; Margaret Orbell and Penguin Books for 'Matai rore au / Love Song'; Bob Orr for 'Shift' and 'Ariel'; Joanna Margaret Paul for extract from 'The Photograph'; Roma Potiki and IWA Associates for 'and my heart goes swimming'; Alan Riach and Auckland University Press for 'The Promise'; Iain Sharp for 'Envoi' and 'At last'; the estate of Helen Shaw for 'The Golden

Flower'; the estate of Keith Sinclair and Auckland University Press for 'The Grin'; Elizabeth Smither for 'The Legend of Marcello Mastroianni's Wife'; Kendrick Smithyman and Auckland University Press for 'Per Diem et per Noctem' and 'Love by Candlelight'; C. K. Stead for extract from 'Uta'; J. C. Sturm for 'A Proposition'; Brian Turner and McIndoe Publishers for 'Like Lamplight'; Hone Tuwhare and Godwit Publishing for 'Thine own hands have fashioned' and 'See what a little moonlight can do to you?'; Ian Wedde and Victoria University Press for 'Beautiful Golden Girl of the Sixties'; Ian Wedde for 'Ruth'; Virginia Were for 'Rangitoto/Canoe'.